KU-638-390

CONTENTS

WHAT ARE EMOTIONS?

We all have emotions that can be positive and negative. But what are emotions exactly?

HOW ARE YOU FEELING?

Take a few seconds to think about the way you're feeling right now. You might say that you feel:

Happy   bored

ANGRY   afraid

EXCITED

sad   lonely

YOUR MIND MATTERS

Your EMOTIONS

Honor Head

W

FRANKLIN WATTS
LONDON • SYDNEY

First published in Great Britain in 2019
by The Watts Publishing Group
10 9 8 7 6 5 4 3 2 1
All rights reserved

Editor: Nicola Edwards
Cover design: Lisa Peacock and Thy Bui
Inside design: Matthew Lilly
Cover and inside illustrations
by Roberta Terracchio
Consultant: Clare Arnold, psychotherapist with 25 years'
experience working with CAMHS, the NHS's Child and
Adolescent Mental Health Services

ISBN 978 1 4451 6469 4 (HB); 978 1 4451 6470 0 (PB)
Printed in China

FSC
www.fsc.org
MIX
Paper from
responsible sources
FSC® C104740

Franklin Watts
An imprint of
Hachette Children's Group
Part of the Watts Publishing Group
Carmelite House
50 Victoria Embankment
London EC4Y 0DZ
An Hachette UK Company
www.hachette.co.uk
www.franklinwatts.co.uk

The website addresses (URLs) included in this book were valid
at the time of going to press. However, it is possible that
contents or addresses may have changed since the publication
of this book. No responsibility for any such changes can be
accepted by either the author or the Publisher.

WHAT IS A TRUSTED ADULT?

Throughout the book we suggest you speak to a trusted adult. This is a person who makes you feel safe and that you can trust. It could be a parent or carer or another family member, such as an aunt or uncle or grandparent. It could be a teacher or someone you know well, such as a family friend or a friend's parent or carer. Or it could be someone at the end of a helpline (see pages 46-47).

These are all emotions. Often we feel a mix of several different emotions at the same time; perhaps we're excited about something that's going to happen, but a little scared as well because it's something new. Maybe we are angry at something a friend did or said, and sad and disappointed that they upset us. Emotions are the feelings we have about the world around us. People, places, school, home, books, films, music, food, clothes, YouTube videos, Instagram, Facebook – everything that is a part of our lives creates an emotion.

EMOTION COMMOTION

Emotions can be lovely. They can make us feel that the world is a wonderful place. They can make us smile and laugh, feel warm and fuzzy inside and dance for joy. But some emotions can make us feel dark and nasty and mean. Sometimes our emotions become overwhelming and we feel we can't control them. They can make us want to do bad things to ourselves or others. They can make us feel that the world is a horrible place and that life is unfair.

LEARNING JOURNEY

Often we can get really confused about how we feel. This is normal as we grow up and have new experiences. As we get older, we learn how different experiences affect us and why we feel good or bad about what other people say or do. We learn how to manage negative emotions and how to express our feelings.

Understanding our emotions can help us to manage our feelings properly. This can help us to make good decisions in life, to control our behaviour and build strong relationships with the people around us. Learning about our emotions and why we feel them can be a really rewarding journey.

TRY THIS!

Look out for these boxes throughout this book. They will give you hints and tips on quick ways to improve your emotional health that you can try every day or whenever you need to.

EMOTIONAL CHAOS

You've probably heard
of puberty and how it affects
your body. Well, it can affect
your mind as well!

HORMONES AND THEIR EFFECTS

As you grow up, and especially when you go through puberty and adolescence, you body changes physically – but so does your mind. Hormones released into your body influence how you feel as well as how you grow. These hormones can affect your emotions, and this can lead to extremes of mood and mood swings. One minute you feel that life is awesome, and the next that it couldn't get any worse!

During puberty your body is dealing with a lot of different physical changes that can make you feel weird or embarrassed. Everyone goes through puberty in their own way. However, if you think your friends might be changing faster or slower than you, this can be frustrating and make you feel 'different' and a bit like an outsider.

WORRYING THOUGHTS

When you go through mood swings you can find yourself fighting with family and friends without really knowing why. You might suddenly feel that no one understands you; this can make you feel alone and rejected. You might even feel that you are going mad, because your mind is whirling with thoughts and feelings that you don't understand and can't control.

IT'S NOT JUST YOU

Feeling like this can be very scary and even though it's your hormones causing havoc, you have to find a way to manage your feelings. Remember that *everyone*, including your teachers, parents and carers, went through something similar at the same age. If you feel really confused and anxious about how you feel, talk to someone. You could speak to an adult you trust at home or at school or even see a doctor who can reassure you that everything is progressing normally.

WHAT ELSE AFFECTS MOODS?

Of course it's not just hormones that affect how we feel. Big and little everyday experiences will cause us to feel different emotions.

PEOPLE POWER

The people around us can affect how we feel. Being with friends and family who love and support us makes us feel happy and confident. If we're with people who make us feel weak and stupid, then we will feel bad about ourselves. Sometimes social media can make us feel sad and lonely and jealous when we see others having a fun time with loads of friends.

LIFESTYLE

What we eat, how well we sleep and how much exercise we do all affect our moods. Experts say you should try to get at least nine to ten hours' sleep a night and eat well. Try to avoid too much sugar and fizzy drinks. Keep yourself hydrated by drinking lots of water throughout the day. If you become dehydrated it can make you feel more grumpy.

Exercise is important, too. It releases feel-good hormones into the body that make us feel better and help to release stress and tension in the body. Even just having a good stretch and jogging on the spot for a few minutes will help relax your body.

TRAUMA

Sometimes very sad things happen. Someone we love dies, or the family splits up, or someone we care about becomes ill. This will be a difficult time for everyone, but especially for young people already being affected by puberty. If something like this happens to you, talk to a teacher, an adult you know well and trust or phone a helpline (see pages 46-47).

You could write down your feelings in a journal or write a poem or a song about how you feel. People often feel angry with a loved one who has died, become ill or left the family – this is a natural reaction and is nothing to feel ashamed of.

"

When Dad left us I was angry with everyone. I blamed Mum, then I blamed Dad. Then I thought it was my fault; I was so confused and scared and sad. Eventually I talked to another girl in my class who was going through the same thing and felt the same way. We both felt better for talking. I'm still sad but I don't feel so alone and scared anymore.

Steph, 11

"

EMOTIONS AND THOUGHTS

Your thoughts can control how you feel so you need to be aware of them.

THOUGHT POWER

Our brain is filled with thoughts that can affect how we feel. Here are some positive thoughts:

I'm really good at maths!

My skin looks great today.

I'm excited about joining the drama group.

Positive thoughts like this help us to feel happy and full of energy. They help us to feel good about ourselves.

Now look at these negative thoughts:

I'm useless at maths.

My skin looks awful.

Nobody in the drama group will think I'm any good.

Negative thoughts make us feel sad
and anxious and bad about ourselves.

FROM BAD TO WORSE

Sometimes people say things that set up a negative
thought that grows and grows. For example, your Dad
might jokingly say that you can't kick a football straight.
This grows in your mind to become 'you're useless at
football' and 'I'm really disappointed in you'.

These negative thoughts have a bad effect on your
self-esteem, or how you see yourself. Before
you know it, you're convinced you're
useless at everything and worthless.

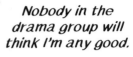

TRAIN YOUR BRAIN

You'll need to be patient, but you can train your brain to be positive. Make a list of all the things you and other people like about you – being kind, good at swimming, and so on. Stick it up in your room where you can see it. When you're feeling bad about yourself, look at your 'likes' list. If you find it hard to shake off your negative feelings, talk to a trusted adult and maybe see a doctor to have a chat about it.

My older sister was always teasing me about my hair saying it was wild and looked a mess. It made me feel awful – I thought everyone was looking at my hair and laughing. I asked my mum if I could cut it all off and we had a long talk about how I felt. She spoke to my sister who had no idea how I felt and said she was sorry she'd upset me. She said she thought I had very pretty hair. I felt much better and started wearing combs and clips in my hair to show it off.

Aisha 10

EMOTIONS AND BEHAVIOUR

Our emotions control how we behave, what we do and say, and how we feel about ourselves and the world around us.

WHY HAVE EMOTIONS?

Emotions play an important part in how we behave in our everyday lives. They affect the decisions we make, how well we do at school and how we treat our family and friends.

Emotions can make us feel good or bad. Sadness, boredom, anger and fear make us feel bad, so we try to avoid them. Happiness, excitement and love make us feel good, so we look for them.

This affects our decision-making and behaviour, as generally we do things to make ourselves and others feel good rather than bad. For example, when we do something that makes someone we care about sad or disappointed we feel guilty. We even feel guilty when we make ourselves feel bad, for example by not doing our homework or by being mean to someone. To avoid feeling guilty again, we do our homework and we're careful not to be mean to anyone. As a result, our dislike of feeling bad has made us behave in a good way.

EMOTIONAL AWARENESS

As we grow up and experience different situations we begin to get better at knowing how ourselves and others are feeling and why. This is called emotional awareness. Being more aware of how we feel and why, helps to develop emotional intelligence. This is an important skill that we will use all our lives.

To develop a healthy emotional awareness you need to be aware of the emotions you feel, and remember when and why you felt them and how you reacted. For example, does a certain song or book make you feel relaxed and inspired or bored and sad? Does being with your friends make you feel happy and excited, or anxious and nervous? By monitoring your feelings you can decide what is good or bad in your life and make changes when you need to.

GET TO KNOW YOUR EMOTIONS

Talk about your feelings to your friends, family, or even your pet, or write about them in a feelings journal. This helps you to express your emotions and to find the words to explain them to yourself and to other people. Don't be afraid of emotions such as anger, frustration, jealousy and fear. Talking honestly about your emotions and thinking about how and why are feeling one way or another can help you to manage these feelings in the future.

SWEATY PALMS AND A RED FACE!

Anxiety and strong emotions, such as anger and fear, can have a physical effect.

ADRENALINE SURGE

Some stressful situations, such as playing in a football match or taking an exam, can make some people feel sick or lightheaded. This is because stress causes a hormone called adrenaline to be pumped around your body.

Adrenaline is released into the body when we feel scared, threatened or very anxious. It is also called the 'fight-or-flight' hormone because it prepares the body to either fight the real or imagined threat or run and escape from it. It does this by contracting blood vessels, making the heart beat faster, restricting air passages and sometimes making you want to go to the loo a lot! Once the scare is over, the adrenaline levels return to normal.

SWEATY PALMS

Lots of people get sweaty palms when they feel anxious or nervous. It often happens if you feel shy or embarrassed in front of other people. It is part of the adrenaline fight-or-flight response to a threatening situation and is perfectly normal. There can also be medical reasons why some people sweat too much. If excessive sweating is stopping you from joining in games, affecting your daily life or making you feel anxious, speak to your parents or carers and ask to see a doctor. If it is being caused by anxiety, it will help to talk to someone about why you are feeling so anxious.

RED FACE

Suddenly blushing, flushing or getting pink or red cheeks is often caused by, yes, you guessed it, adrenaline! Talking to new people or standing in front of an audience makes lots of people feel anxious or nervous. This creates an adrenaline surge that makes blood rush to the face, causing blushing.

When we meet new people we want them to like us and so subconsciously we are thinking about what impression we are making. This feeling of nervousness can cause us to blush.

TRY THIS!

Next time you are in a situation that makes you blush, take a deep breath and breathe out slowly. Focus on the people you are talking to and what you think about them. That way you'll stop thinking about yourself.

FEELING SAD

Everyone feels sad
at times and it's perfectly
normal to have sad feelings.

WHAT MAKES US FEEL SAD?

Some things in life make us sad, from a weepy film, a good friend moving away, or something really big like the death of a relative or a family break-up. Some sad feelings only last for a short time, while others can be very painful and last for a very long time.

Sadness can also make us feel lonely. It can isolate us from other people who are having a good time and make us feel alone.

In most cases we can do things to help us to feel better when we are sad, but sometimes the sadness is just too great and can be overwhelming. Talk to someone about why you feel so sad. It might help to have a good cry. Keep a journal about your sadness – but don't share what you write online. Keep these personal thoughts private. Drawing and painting can sometimes help us to express our sadness especially when we can't talk about it. Even the worst sadness you can think of gets easier to cope with over time.

HOW TO COPE

Learning to understand and manage your emotions is part of becoming an adult. For example, if you've done badly in an exam you can choose to learn from what went wrong and be determined to do better next time.

If one of your friends doesn't want to talk to you any more, see it as their loss and look for other friends that you can trust, or join a new club to do more of a hobby you enjoy. Disappointment and failure can make you feel sad, but can also be opportunities to try something new and be better.

TRY THIS!

🙂 *Think about things that have made you feel proud, such as winning a race or being praised for your schoolwork.*

🙂 *Focus on something else. Offer to help in the kitchen or plan a makeover for your room.*

🙂 *Sometimes spending too much time online can make people feel isolated. Get together with some friends and go for a walk or have a game in the park.*

🙂 *When you exercise your body releases feel-good hormones called endorphins into your brain. Try swimming, tennis, football, trampolining, or a dance class to make you feel better ... and you'll be fitter, too.*

DEPRESSION

There are different levels of sadness and sometimes feeling sad can become something more serious that needs medical help. If you feel sad for a long time, feel irritable and grumpy all the time, lose interest in being with your friends, can't be bothered with schoolwork, sleep more or can't sleep at all, feel tired and exhausted and have thoughts about harming yourself, you may be suffering from depression. Speak to your parents or carers and ask to see your doctor who will give you professional advice. Don't leave it and hope it will go away; ask for help.

FEELING HAPPY

We all want to be happy
and often it is the smallest things
that make us truly content.

CAN'T BUY HAPPINESS

It sounds boring, but it's true: you can't buy happiness.
It might make you feel good when you buy a new pair
of trainers or the latest video game, but the feeling
doesn't last. Scientific research has shown that shopping
releases feel-good hormones into the brain, but this
feeling only lasts for a short while. You then have to buy
something else to feel the same way again.

Feeling truly happy comes from how you live your life, how you treat others and how you feel about yourself and the world. Being with people you love and who love you back, being kind, caring and having people care for you, are the things that make us truly content.

MAKE YOURSELF HAPPY

Most of the time, unless there's a medical reason why you feel sad (see page 24), you have the power to make yourself happy. It hurts when people are mean to you and it is disappointing if you can't buy what you really want, but you can control how you deal with these emotions.

You can believe the mean things people say or you can ignore them and walk away. You can feel angry and upset that you can't buy what you want, or you can think of ways to make some extra pocket money so that you can save up to buy what you want. Taking control of your emotions and behaving in a positive way helps to make you feel strong and increases your self-esteem, which makes you feel good about yourself and happy!

FRIENDS!

Having good friends helps to keep us feeling positive and stops us feeling sad and lonely. Good friends are kind, respectful and loyal. And remember, being 'popular' isn't the same as having good friends. Having one or two really close friends that you trust is worth more than having lots of friends who hang around with you but don't really care about you.

"When my mum and dad split up I was so angry and scared. I was really mean to my best mate, but he knew what was going on at home and stood by me. One day we were playing football and I blurted out how I felt. I still don't know what's going to happen, but I feel a lot better knowing my mate is there for me and that he's not judging me.

Ryan, 14

FEELING ANGRY

We all feel angry at
times and that's fine;
it's how we deal with our
anger that's important.

AAARGH!

There are lots of reasons why we feel angry. It could be
when someone says something that is wrong or mean.
Or it could be when you think that life is being unfair.
Maybe you feel angry when you want to do something
and your parents say 'no', or when you try to learn
something new and struggle to get it right.

Some anger is good, for
example if someone is
being bullied at school it
is right to get angry and
tell a teacher. It's how
we behave when we're
dealing with feelings of
anger that's important.

DEAL WITH IT

Try and deal calmly with what made you angry or hurt you. Speak to the person who upset you or if you feel frustrated with schoolwork, talk to a teacher about it. At home, think about what makes you angry, but instead of expressing your frustration, ask the adults for a time when you can sit down and talk when they can give you their full attention. Tell them calmly why you feel angry and then listen to what they say to you. See if you can solve the issues in a grown-up way that will make you all feel better about the situation.

DON'T LOSE IT!

Sometimes stress about school or home can build up until we feel like exploding. If you feel like this try not to shout, scream, be abusive or lash out. Losing your temper and being aggressive or violent will only make any situation much, much worse. If you can, walk away from what has made you angry. Find somewhere quiet – in the garden, an empty classroom – anywhere that is a safe space. Take deep breaths and slowly count to ten. If you can, punch a pillow, scream into a cushion, stamp your feet and clench and unclench your fists.

DON'T BE A BULLY

If you are taking your anger out on other people by bullying or being nasty, think about why you are angry. If someone is bullying you or making you feel ashamed or bad about yourself, you need to talk to someone you trust about it. Taking your anger out on other people will only make you feel worse about yourself and could get you into trouble.

FEELING SCARED

Everyone feels scared sometimes and this is not necessarily a bad thing. Fear can be a destructive emotion, but it can be useful, too.

FEELING FEAR

We feel afraid when we don't know what's going to happen or when we think something bad is going happen. We should listen to our fear when it is a warning not to do something dangerous, but how can we deal with fear when it stops us doing things that might be good for us?

AFRAID TO FAIL

A fear of failure means we avoid trying new things in case we don't get them right or make a fool of ourselves trying. Everyone feels like this sometimes, even adults, and the truth is that some of the most successful people in the world from singers to business billionaires have made plenty of mistakes along the way. If we do our best but still fail it can be a good thing. Failing teaches us the right way to do something or to try a different way. We can all learn from failure. When you do fail don't think you're a loser and useless, think positive thoughts about how you can make it work next time.

ANXIETY

Anxiety is when you feel worried, nervous and scared to try something because you don't know what might happen. It could be meeting new people or sitting an exam, for example. When you get anxious you might be aware of a fluttery feeling in your tummy, your heart might beat faster and you might start to sweat more. Remember everyone gets anxious at times, so it's not just you.

FROM FEAR TO PHOBIA

Sometimes a fear we have can develop into something more serious. A phobia is when a person becomes too terrified to do something, for example being afraid to leave their home in case something terrible happens to them outside.

If you have a phobia that is affecting your day-to-day life, talk to an adult you trust about it and seek medical help. A doctor or specialist will be able help you deal with the phobia. Don't think you're being weak or silly by asking for help; it's a very brave thing to do.

> *My panic attacks started when I was nine. I would shake and sweat and feel like being sick. I couldn't breathe and felt like I was being smothered. My mum took me to see a specialist and it really helped. I am okay at school now and can go out with friends. At last my life is getting back to normal.*
>
> Jake, 15

RELATIONSHIPS

The relationships we have
throughout our lives have a
very important effect on how
we feel about ourselves
and the world around us.

CONNECTIONS

A relationship is an emotional connection between
two or more people. Our first relationships are with
our family – the adults who look after us, brothers and
sisters, aunts, uncles, grandparents and cousins.

As we get older we start to develop friendships and relationships with people outside the family, such as classmates and teachers. Later, we will have relationships with lots of people, including people we work with. Building caring, supportive relationships throughout our lives is very important to our physical and mental wellbeing.

MIXED EMOTIONS

All relationships are based on emotions. The emotions can be positive, such as love, joy and excitement, or negative, such as hate, anger and sadness. Most relationships are a mix of all these emotions. We love and care for our family and friends, but often get angry with them or feel sad if we feel they've let us down.

This is completely normal and healthy if we can talk about what has upset us and then move on. In a strong relationship the positive emotions are much stronger than the negative ones and communication between you stays open and honest whatever happens.

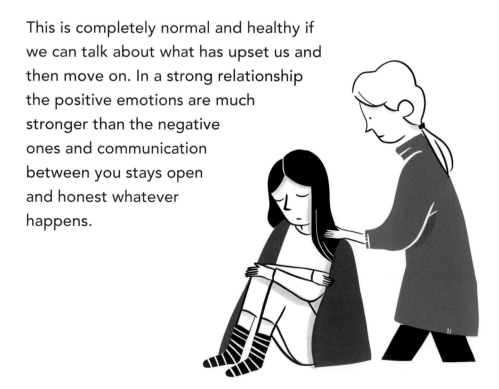

GOOD FEELINGS

If someone has a caring, loving and supportive family they feel happier, more confident and have higher self-esteem. If their family is always arguing, or being nasty to each other, this makes them feel miserable and can affect their self-esteem and schoolwork. If a sibling or adult at home is making you feel scared or bad about yourself, you don't have to put up with it just because you are a child. Speak to a trusted adult who will be able to help you decide what to do or call a helpline (see pages 46-47). Every child has the right to feel safe and cared for at home.

"

My older sister was really sad because her boyfriend had broken up with her. We haven't always been best friends, but I hated seeing her like that. One day I went and sat with her and held her hand and took her my favourite teddy. We didn't say anything; she just cried and I hugged her. Later she said that made her feel much better and how lucky she was to have such a kind sister. I felt so pleased and proud that I'd been able to help her.

Poppy, 10

"

FRIENDS FOR LIFE

Friends are a very
important part of your life
so it's important to know how
to be a good friend.

A good friend:

* praises and compliments
  you when you've done
  something special
* hugs and comforts you
  when things go wrong
* supports and encourages
  you to do your best
* listens to you and shares
  their own feelings with you
* is someone you can trust
  and rely on to be
  there for you and
  who makes you
  feel happy and
  good about
  yourself.

WHAT IS EMPATHY?

As young people get older and start to go through puberty, they usually become more aware of how other people feel and react to them. They develop a sense of empathy. Empathy is when we understand and share other people's emotions and feelings. For example, if a friend is having a tough time at home, you can see how sad or angry the friend is. You understand how your friend is feeling even though you aren't feeling that emotion yourself. Because of this you can comfort your friend and try and make them feel better, or just be there for them.

Sometimes your feeling of empathy might be so strong you find that you feel angry for your friend or that their sadness makes you cry. This works with good feelings, too. If a friend has passed an exam or won a sport's match, you can feel really happy for them.

OH, NO! FRENEMIES!

These are the opposite of good friends. They are people who say they are your friend, but they put you down all the time. They laugh if you make a mistake and jeer if you get something right. They can be jealous and nasty.

Everyone deserves to have good friends so take steps to put things right. Talk to the friend who is upsetting you the most. If they are sorry and feel bad about what they've done, you can decide to give them another chance.

If they laugh and call you names, you need to drop them. They were never true friends at all and you'll be happier finding new friends. This is not easy to do, but it will increase your self-esteem to know that you took steps to make yourself feel better.

MAKING NEW FRIENDS

Not everyone makes friends easily; we can all feel a bit scared of being rejected or ignored sometimes, but remember, everyone feels the same. Join a club or group to meet people who share the same interests. Sit near a group of people you like or go up to someone sitting alone and say hello to them. You never know, this could be your new best friend!

THE LAST WORD ... ME!

Be your own best friend
and find out what makes you
feel the best you can.

KNOW 'ME'

Take some time to think about what makes you happy
and excited, what you look forward to and who you
enjoy being with. Keeping a journal of your feelings can
often help to pinpoint what made you feel anxious and
worried or joyful and pleased. Once you know what
triggers your different emotions, you can do more to
encourage the good ones and avoid the bad ones.

FORGIVE 'ME'

We all do and say
things we regret, but
what is important is
what we do about
it afterwards.

Saying sorry, explaining why you behaved the way you did and making sure not to do it again, is a very grown up and brave thing to do. Above all, forgive yourself. Don't end up feeling guilty about what you did and thinking you're a bad person and don't allow other people to make you feel guilty. These are negative feelings that can affect your whole outlook, but only if you let them.

LOVE 'ME'

Try to fill your life with as many positive emotions as you can by being caring and kind to others. Make a point to have a go at learning new skills and having new experiences. Believe that you are valuable and worthwhile, and know that you are unique and special and deserve happiness and love.

GLOSSARY

ABUSIVE
insulting, aggressive
and nasty

ADOLESCENCE
the period following
puberty, when a young
person develops into
an adult

ANXIOUS
feeling worried, uneasy
or uncertain

COMPLIMENTS
things people say that
praise you

DEHYDRATED
dry and thirsty;
needing water

DEPRESSION
a mental state when
a person feels sad, unable
to get involved or do
anything and
feels worthless

EMOTIONAL AWARENESS
being aware of your feelings
and what makes you feel
that way

EMOTIONAL INTELLIGENCE
being able to recognise
your emotions and why you
feel them, and knowing how
to cope with them

EMPATHY
being able to understand
and share other people's
feelings

FRUSTRATION
a feeling of being upset
or annoyed because
something isn't going as
you had planned

HORMONES
chemical substances
released into your body
that affect how you grow
and how you feel

HYDRATED
having plenty of water

NEGATIVE
describes a gloomy, dark
feeling that things can't
be done

POSITIVE
describes a confident, good
feeling that things will work
out fine

PUBERTY
the time when your body
is growing and changing
into an adult body

SELF-ESTEEM
confidence in yourself;
belief in your own worth
and your abilities

SIBLINGS
brothers and sisters

SUBCONSCIOUSLY
happening in your mind
without you being aware

NOTES FOR TEACHERS, PARENTS AND CARERS

It is important to encourage positive emotions in young people at all times, at home and at school and to be aware of youngsters who may be suffering from negative emotions. At school and home, teaching children skills in how to deal with emotions is crucial. Assertiveness skills, problem solving and conflict resolving skills help young people to take control of their lives and help them to manage challenging emotions.

TEACHERS, LOOK OUT FOR:
* students becoming withdrawn and hunched
* changes or fluctuations in behaviour or attitudes
* usually calm students becoming aggressive, angry or confrontational
* students being diffident about their work, not really trying or skipping classes.

WHAT TO DO:
* Discuss emotions in class. Use this book as a basis to discuss how students feel and how they handle their emotions.
* Talk about the different situations that provoke different emotions. Try role playing or writing a class play about emotions.

* If a student is displaying signs of extreme emotion, such as anger or sadness, take them aside and have a quiet word, such as saying you noticed that they look/seem angry/sad. Empathise with them and try to find out what has caused the mood and discuss with them what can be done about it.
* Think about setting up an emotions space. This could be an empty classroom that is supervised at certain times, such as during the lunch break. It could be a place where students can go to write down how they feel. It gives them a quiet, safe space to explore their feelings by themselves. The teacher is on hand to talk if needed.
* Ask students to take an assembly about different emotions.

FOR PARENTS AND CARERS

All pre-teens and teenagers will go through emotional phases of being grumpy, aggressive, frustrated and withdrawn. Within reason, this is normal. Talk to your child about their feelings. Listen to what they say. Empathise with them. This way they learn that feelings can be discussed and not hidden away, ignored or repressed. They also begin to accept that bad feelings will go away.

If your child misbehaves because of feelings of anger, disappointment or frustration, explain that it is the bad behaviour that is unacceptable, not the feeling.

Go through this book with your child and discuss the issues. Ask questions gently to encourage your child to open up and let them take the lead in the conversation.

If you feel your child is excessively angry, defiant, resentful and abusive or overly withdrawn and timid, or if there is a big change in your child's outlook and behaviour, such as not eating, excessive eating, over sleeping or insomnia, either phone a helpline (see pages 46-47) or contact your doctor.

FURTHER INFORMATION

WEBSITES AND HELPLINES

If you feel overwhelmed by any of the issues you've read about in this book, or need advice, check out a website or call a helpline and talk to someone who will understand.

www.childline.org.uk/info-advice/your-feelings/mental-health
Message or call the 24-hour helpline for advice or someone who'll just listen.
The helpline number is 0800 1111.

www.samaritans.org
A place where anyone can go for advice and comfort. The helpline number is 116 123.

www.sane.org/get-help
Help and support for anyone affected by mental and emotional issues.
The helpline number is 0300 304 7000.

www.supportline.org.uk
A charity giving emotional support to young people.
The helpline number is 01708 765200.

kidshealth.org/en/kids/feeling
Advice on managing emotions.

https://www.brainline.org/article/who-me-self-esteem-people-disabilities
How to boost self-esteem regardless of disabilities.

www.youngminds.org.uk
Advice for young people experiencing bullying, stress and mental or emotional anxieties.

FOR PARENTS AND CARERS

www.healthyplace.com
Information on depression and other emotional issues and advice on how to help someone going through depression.

kidshealth.org/en/parents/emotions
How to recognise an emotional phase or something more serious. Advice on how to help your child cope with emotional issues.

AUSTRALIA AND NEW ZEALAND

www.healthdirect.gov.au/partners/kids-helpline
A helpline for young people giving advice,
counselling and support.
The number is 1800 55 1800.

www.kidsline.org.nz
Helpline run by specially trained young
volunteers to help kids and teens deal with troubling
issues and problems.
The number is 0800 54 37 54.

Note to parents and teachers: every effort has been made by the
Publishers to ensure that these websites are suitable for children,
that they are of the highest educational value, and that they
contain no inappropriate or offensive material. However, because
of the nature of the Internet, it is impossible to guarantee that the
contents of these sites will not be altered. We strongly advise that
Internet access is supervised by a responsible adult.

BOOKS

Positively Teenage
by Nicola Morgan, Franklin Watts, 2018

*You Are Awesome: Find Your Confidence and
Dare to be Brilliant at (Almost) Anything*
by Matthew Syed, Wren & Rook, 2018

*Hello Happy! Mindful Kids: An activity book
for young people who sometimes feel
sad or angry*
by Katie Abey, Studio Press, 2017

◀ The Argentinian rugby team (in blue) play against other teams from around the world, such as Australia.

Many people in Argentina like to play football and rugby. They also watch football and rugby matches.

Argentinian football fans cheered for their team at the 2014 World Cup. ▼

Do you have a favourite sports team? Which team is it and why do you support them?

15

Festivals

In March, people in the city of Mendoza **celebrate** the grape **harvest**. There are parades in the streets.

These boys are playing music in a parade to celebrate the grape harvest.

16

In August, there is a tango festival
in Buenos Aires. The tango is
a traditional dance from Argentina.
It is a dance for two people.

▲ During the tango festival, dancers perform in the street.

Wildlife

Animals such as guanacos and foxes live in the grasslands and mountains of Argentina.

▼ Guanacos eat grass and other plants.

Which birds live in your country?

◄ Flamingos live in lakes in Argentina. They eat tiny animals and plants that live in the water.

Different birds live in lakes and on the coast of Argentina.

Penguins come to the south coast of Argentina. They lay their eggs and look after their chicks there. ▼

People

Lionel Messi is a football player from Argentina. He is the captain of the Argentinian football team.

Messi played football for Barcelona Football Club in Spain for 21 years. ▼

20

Pope Francis is the **leader** of the **Catholic Church**. He was born in Argentina.

◀ Pope Francis wears special robes and a necklace with a crucifix on it.

crucifix

Quiz

Test how much you remember.

Check your answers on page 24.

1 Name a country that is next to Argentina.

2 What is the capital of Argentina?

3 What is a gaucho?

4 What is mate made from?

5 When is the grape harvest festival?

6 Who is Lionel Messi?

Glossary

Atlantic Ocean – the ocean between the east of North and South America and the west of Europe and Africa

border – the line that divides two countries

cable car – a vehicle that is pulled on thick wires

capital city – the city where a country's government work

Catholic Church – the part of the Christian religion that has the Pope as its leader

celebrate – to do something fun on a special day

coast – the land by the sea

country – an area of land that has its own government

glacier – a large block of ice that moves very slowly between mountains

grassland – a large area of land covered in grass

harvest – when crops are ready to be picked

laws – the rules of a country that everyone has to follow

leader – the person in charge of something

South America – a continent that includes countries such as Brazil, Argentina and Venezuela

traditional – describes something that has been done in the same way for many years

www.southdublinlibraries.ie South Dublin Libraries

Index

Answers:

1: Brazil, Chile, Uruguay, Paraguay, Bolivia; 2: Buenos Aires; 3: An Argentinian farmer who rides a horse; 4: Plant leaves and hot water; 5: March; 6: An Argentinian footballer

Teaching notes:

Children who are reading Book band Purple or above should be able to enjoy this book with some independence. Other children will need more support.

Before you share the book:

- Show children different world maps and globes. Ensure they understand that blue represents sea and other colours show the land.
- Help them to orientate their understanding of the globe by pointing out where Argentina is in relation to North America, Africa and Antarctica.
- Talk about what they already know about South America and Argentina.

While you share the book:

- Help children to read some of the more unfamiliar words.
- Talk about the questions. Encourage children to make links between their own experiences and the information in the book.
- Compare the information about Argentina with where you live. What is the same? What is different?

After you have shared the book:

- Talk about the weather in Argentina. What do children know about the weather in Brazil (to the north) and Antarctica (to the south)? How would this help them to predict weather in Argentina?
- Challenge children to find out more about gauchos and their lifestyle.
- Work through the free activity sheets at www.hachetteschools.co.uk